RAISING COMPASSIONATE KIDS

RAISING COMPASSIONATE KIDS

HANLEY STANLEY

CONTENTS

1 Introduction to Compassionate Parenting   1
2 Core Principle 1: Modeling Compassionate Behavior   5
3 Core Principle 2: Teaching Empathy and Perspective   9
4 Core Principle 3: Encouraging Acts of Kindness and   13
5 Core Principle 4: Fostering a Positive and Inclusi   17
6 Core Principle 5: Setting Boundaries and Consisten   21
7 The Role of Communication in Compassionate Parenti 23
8 Cultivating Resilience and Self-Compassion in Chil   27
9 Navigating Challenges and Obstacles in Parenting w   31
10 Celebrating Diversity and Promoting Inclusivity in   35
11 The Importance of Self-Care for Parents in Raising   39
12 Conclusion: Embracing the Journey of Compassionate 41

Copyright © 2024 by Hanley Stanley
All rights reserved. No part of this book may be reproduced in any manner whatsoever without written permission except in the case of brief quotations embodied in critical articles and reviews.
First Printing, 2024

CHAPTER 1

Introduction to Compassionate Parenting

What does it mean to be compassionate? We can all recognize a compassionate person when we see them. They are patient when we tell the same stories over and over again. They offer to help us when we have to move, or when we can't walk the dog tonight because we're feeling sick. They're ready with a reassuring hug when we just can't seem to master something that seems to come so easily to everyone else.

Raising compassionate kids is about more than teaching them how to identify a feeling in someone else and react to it. Being a compassionate family is about breathing in the world's pain and acting to alleviate it, one small corner of the world at a time. It can be hard to define exactly what a compassionate family looks like, but we intuitively know one when we see—or meet—one. Compassionate families stand out.

For me, these five core values and practices of compassionate families are what make them so special. As I've worked, talked, and laughed with families who seem to catch on to this whole being-a-completely-decent-human-being thing, these traits, too, seem to be core to their character. The parents who seem to move through their day in a very intentional way are unapologetically compassionate. They all define it a little differently, but true, measured, compassionate behavior is a goal that resonates deeply with all kinds of families.

Here are the five core values that I believe are crucial for compassionate families:

1. **Compassion is a Learning Process.**
2. **True Compassionate Behavior Comes from Inside of Us, Not from External Rewards.**
3. **Parenting with Compassion Can Feel Overwhelming, but It's Necessary.**
4. **Compassionate Parenting is Peaceful Relational Work.**
5. **Both Adults and Kids Must Believe that Other People Care About Their Feelings in Order to Truly Access Their Empathy.**

Defining Compassion in the Context of Parenting

Compassion is a fundamental value exemplified by relational bonds. Within the context of parenting, compassion is conceptualized as an attitudinal and behavioral expression of loving-kindness for a child. It combines a focus on the child's emotions and experiences with a desire to help, an orientation toward understanding the child's experiences, and a commitment to helping the child cope and make changes in their behavior.

Compassion is a response to children's suffering, whether it is distress, sadness, fear, anger, or even happiness. Such a response to children can help cultivate secure, dependable, and kind values from which further developmental potential can be harvested. At a deep existential level, compassion empowers a child to task manage, find internal motivation, trust, and be responsive within a new gestalt of interpenetrating inside and outside worlds.

Parenting is fundamental in guiding a child away from harm and exploitation and toward physical and psychological well-being. Parents model values, provide acceptance, and actively rear children toward reaching and manifesting their potentials in their adult lives. Compassionate parents attempt to understand their children's feelings and perspectives and are equally quick to signal their care.

In this section, the five core principles of parenting based on compassionate care are outlined. These include the principles of **Care**, **Clarity**, **Commitment**, **Consistency**, and **Creative Conflict Resolution**.

Expanding Each Principle:

1. **Care**:
    - Demonstrating care involves active listening, empathizing with your child's feelings, and validating their emotions.
    - Care also includes attending to your child's physical needs, offering comfort, and creating a safe and nurturing environment.
    - Practical ways to show care: Daily check-ins, family routines, and dedicated quality time.
2. **Clarity**:
    - Clarity means setting clear expectations, boundaries, and guidelines for behavior.
    - It also involves communicating with your child in a straightforward and understandable manner.
    - Practical ways to maintain clarity: Consistent rules, clear instructions, and open discussions about values and expectations.
3. **Commitment**:

- Being committed to your child's well-being involves being there for them consistently, showing reliability, and following through on promises.
- It's about being dedicated to their growth and supporting them through challenges.
- Practical ways to show commitment: Consistent support in their activities, being present during important moments, and making time for bonding.

4. **Consistency**:
    - Consistency in parenting helps children feel secure and understand the consequences of their actions.
    - It's about being predictable in your responses and maintaining a stable environment.
    - Practical ways to maintain consistency: Regular routines, consistent discipline, and stable family traditions.

5. **Creative Conflict Resolution**:
    - This principle involves teaching children how to handle conflicts constructively and find solutions that work for everyone involved.
    - It includes fostering problem-solving skills, empathy, and cooperation.
    - Practical ways to practice creative conflict resolution: Role-playing conflict scenarios, discussing feelings and solutions, and encouraging teamwork and compromise.

CHAPTER 2

Core Principle 1: Modeling Compassionate Behavior

Numerous studies show how children are predisposed to care about others and act with kindness and cooperation from early on in life. Their compassionate disposition is particularly shaped through the ways in which caregivers respond and model compassion in their everyday lives. As role models for their children, parents' compassion and empathy toward each other, as well as toward their children, are associated with the development of prosocial attitudes and behaviors in their offspring. Even before the time of parental human agentic influences, infants are exposed to a warm and nurturing environment. Over time, the values and attitudes of parents as role models can shape both a child's moral foundation and behavior.

Core Principle Elaboration: Lead by Example

Different from explicitly teaching children about compassion, Core Principle 1 emphasizes the key role of the parent as a model of compassionate behavior. In the early years, a child is impressionable and learns through observation and imitation. As early as infancy, the ability to adapt to others' mental and emotional states is being built through the gentle holding of a caregiver. Parents are the first and primary teachers for showing developing little ones how to care for and listen with an open heart to the diverse emotions and needs of others. By helping our children form a foundation for compassion, they can call upon it in times big and small because it is often from moments of small sacrifices and inhibiting self-interest that growth is born.

Leading by Example

Modeling compassionate living for kids involves leading by example. The way parents act toward and talk to others is incredibly influential for kids. They listen not just to the ideas, values, and social expectations that are expressed to them, but to the ones parents and other authority figures seem to live by. When there's a contradiction between words and actions, they're more likely to listen to and be influenced by the latter. That's why one of the most powerful things parents can do is to lead by example, treating others and their kids with patience, kindness, and civility. This doesn't mean being a perfect parent, but it does mean having a deeply considered approach to your parenting and consistently showing good faith in furthering core principles.

It's in our moment-to-moment interactions with our kids that we create the emotional and psychological environment that helps them accept, learn, and then live in the ways parents are hoping. Here are a few things to keep in mind to demonstrate compassionate living through our parenting:

1. **Consistency Between Words and Actions**:
    - The alignment between what's said and what's done is essential. It's not just about sending a one-off message about generosity or empathy. It's about building a per-

spective in the kids that the values you are talking about are the right ones and can be used to navigate the world.
- If you say that being considerate is important and show it to other people, kids are much more likely to think that other people also care about this value and see it as a reasonable one to guide their behavior.

2. **Modeling Daily Actions**:
   - Actions, done consistently over time, serve as a great way for parents to provide a model of what it is to be a good adult.
   - Simple acts of kindness, patience, and empathy in everyday interactions can leave a lasting impact on children.

3. **Creating a Supportive Environment**:
   - An emotionally and psychologically supportive environment helps kids feel safe and understood, making it easier for them to adopt compassionate behaviors.
   - Encouraging open communication, validating their feelings, and showing unconditional love are key components.

By leading by example, parents do much of their best parenting. The consistent demonstration of compassionate behavior not only teaches children valuable life skills but also helps in creating a compassionate and empathetic future generation.

CHAPTER 3

Core Principle 2: Teaching Empathy and Perspective

Teaching empathy and perspective-taking is the second principle of the five core principles of raising compassionate children. Ingraining empathy is possible when kids have a clear idea of what emotions are and are able to recognize them in others. By discussing emotions openly, we show that they are important and can be better understood. Once kids are able to recognize them in themselves, they can recognize emotions in others. We can encourage empathy by discussing and explaining how other people might feel in a given situation. We can also discuss how others might interpret a given situation in contrast to how we view it ourselves. Once kids have a strong understanding of perspective-taking, they can also learn to be sensitive when expressing themselves, knowing that what they may need to express could hurt someone's feelings. Lastly, we can teach our children that they can show care and concern towards others to make the people around them feel better. If we continuously encourage expressions of care, they will eventually become a habit.

Perspective-taking is important in becoming a child's first foundation in their journey to compassion. If children can develop a strong sense of understanding from someone else's perspective, they can be well on their way to developing an active sense of concern and interest in bettering the experiences of those around them. The core of empathy includes an understanding of emotions and the ability to take someone else's perspective. Whereas sympathy is merely the feeling of an emotion, empathy is the alignment of concern in making things better.

Core Principle Elaboration: Teaching Empathy and Perspective-Taking

The age of reflection toward mainstream individualism has produced a stigma against the use of the word empathy. Its synonymous usage with the word "sympathy" and the connotations associated with it have been so negative in our current vocabulary that the common use of the word empathy as a form of mediation has been forgotten. Empathy and compassion are not deeply biological programs but involve multiple processes failing to communicate simply and elegantly with one another.

Developing Emotional Intelligence

Emotional Intelligence: Empathy and Perspective-Taking

A major component of creating a compassionate climate is teaching emotional intelligence. Emotional intelligence encompasses the skills of empathy, peaceful conflict resolution, and solving interpersonal problems. The most essential part of emotional intelligence is empathy. Empathy includes having the perspective-taking abilities described above. With this skill, we are able to see from another person's point of view. We think about their feelings and experiences as well as our own.

Empathy grows as we become more emotionally literate. When we can label what we or another person is feeling, we have a new level of control. This level of control, in turn, advances our ability to be empathic or compassionate. To heighten compassionate actions in children, parents need to help them build a varied vocabulary in feeling words, recognize their own and others' feelings with these words, and learn to cope and solve problems or introduce alternative behaviors resulting in compassionate action.

Emotional intelligence is fundamental for parents to understand as we attempt to teach our children empathy. Both emotional intelligence and empathy are consciously chosen expressions of our love. A growing number of resources, courses, and studies are available in emotional literacy exercises at local universities and schools. Scholarly journals contain many studies showing a direct correlation between emotional intelligence and both educational success and general success in the workforce. Many feel that, as adults, if they became more developed in this area, their children's lives would benefit equally.

Although some children are born more empathic than others, there are a variety of nurturance techniques and exercises that can help foster children's compassionate nature. It is possible that children often feel what others feel because they can easily imitate the vocal tones and facial expressions of others to build or decrease empathy. Even when children are born with some of these tendencies toward empathy, this trait needs to be nurtured to become stronger. Parents need to be direct in accelerating their child's development in this area. Helping children to develop a sense of empathy and sensitivity may be more important than any skills that can be taught.

CHAPTER 4

Core Principle 3: Encouraging Acts of Kindness and

Encouraging acts of kindness and service is the third principle of the five core principles of raising compassionate children. We can do a better job of raising compassionate children. A pervasive assumption has been that empathy is either present or absent, while the most recent research suggests it is more like a muscle that, when exercised, grows. Once parents understand the importance of nurturing empathy in their children, their assumption is that compassion and the desire to serve will follow naturally.

The principle of service applies to all ages and abilities. Service can be seen operating as a powerful teaching tool for social responsibility inside classrooms, in the belief that acting like a compassionate person will lead children to become kind people. This value of service, along with all of the other five core principles, guides the "Language of Compassion" program developed in the Tacoma public schools. "We believe that ultimately wanting to relieve the suffering of others, helping them rise from their place of sorrow, leads to acts of kindness." Educators at the Search Institute, taking a different path, link each fundamental moral value to a skill and to opportunities for instruction. For example, the value of compassion is seen as showing concern for others, talking about how it feels to be left out, and practicing helping those who are bullied. According to the Institute, truly "caring children" (those who exhibit compassion) are also motivated to become responsible citizens.

Altruism—the unselfish desire to help others—is a different construct from compassion. Normatively, altruism would be more similar to the idea of service, where compassion would be on a par with other ideas and attitudes. In this way, altruism fits the morals and values on the left-hand side of Wilson's schema, while compassion is nested in the middle, within what Wilson terms "virtue." Altruism includes collecting teddy bears for children in a war-torn country or donating money for meals. Care consists of kindness-related ideas, such as feeling concern for those treated poorly or who are sick.

Core Principle Elaboration: Encouraging Acts of Kindness and Service

Teaching empathy alone is not enough. We must actively encourage our children to perform acts of kindness and service. This encourages them to practice empathy in tangible ways and see the direct impact their actions can have on others. By incorporating these activities into their lives, we help foster a sense of social responsibility and build a compassionate character.

Volunteering as a Family

Volunteering as a family is a powerful way to show that we care about others and are in touch with the deeper, more compassionate side of life. When children volunteer, they feel valuable and competent. They are part of a community, meet people from various backgrounds, share experiences, and identify with those who have less, all while sharing the warmth and compassion of the nurturing adults in their lives.

Here are a few family-friendly volunteer activities to consider:

- **Make and deliver a turkey sandwich to a homeless person**: Explain the importance of charity and helping others.
- **Check the local newspaper for family-friendly volunteer opportunities**: Look for activities where children can be involved, such as reading tutoring, coaching sports, or fundraising for a local cause.
- **Participate in charity drives**: Collect items like teddy bears for children in need or donations for local food banks.

Before initiating family activities, check with local agencies for age-appropriate volunteer opportunities. Some organizations may have age restrictions to ensure safety and manage emotional overstimulation for younger children.

By modeling the charity ethic and inviting children to participate at their level, parents can instill a lasting sense of compassion and service in their children.

CHAPTER 5

Core Principle 4: Fostering a Positive and Inclusi

Creating a nurturing environment is critical to foster the development, sustainment, and generalization of pro-social behaviors in family members. It is difficult to share and care when bombarded by negativity. Environments that convey empathy, respect, and inclusivity support the development of warm-heartedness in family members. When children feel respected, accepted, and heard, they are more likely to extend the same positive attention to others.

Our formal definition of creating a world of kindness starts in our home. A research article completed by David Hamilton (a post-doc fellow at the core lab at Northeastern) that appeared in the Scientific American in 2018 identified empathy, compassion, and the overall well-being of family members can be positively impacted through a change in the dynamics in most households. These dynamics included inclusivity and emotional sharing space within the household. Specifically for nurturing love and kindness in children, Hamilton argued that "in order to raise more compassionate and caring children, parents may need to re-evaluate and re-configure some of the ways they are approaching parenting." With their empathetic and creative qualities, choosing to follow in the spirit of Hamilton's argument, our team has developed 5 Core Principles of Parenting. The table below will outline these 5 Core Principles. Today's focus is on Core Principle #4.

CORE PRINCIPLES OF PARENTING:

- Principle #1: Becoming compassionate grown-ups is the most important thing our children will ever do!
- Principle #2: Leading by example speaks volumes to our children - words make the music, the inherent melody is someone else's empathy.
- Principle #3: Creating a world of kindness begins at home!
- Principle #4: Nurturing compassion is our responsibility!
- Principle #5: Encouraging compassion in our children is not always obvious, so look for teachable moments.

Creating a Culture of Acceptance

Embrace your child's individuality by celebrating their unique qualities and differences. This may include differences in IQ and academic success if your child does not fit the traditional academic mold, physical differences, and more. Parents often pit kids against each other by praising one child, often the most athletic or academically successful, and using this praise as a measuring stick against siblings and peers.

Promote understanding and compassion for others in your child's social circle by modeling and teaching respect for differences that others may have. It is important to create a home and family culture that focuses on differences and diversity as a strength because it encourages an appreciation of self, too. Encourage your child to identify one unique thing about themselves that they bring to their group of friends. Childhood and the teenage years are a time when acceptance and belonging within social groups is often paramount. Help your child to see the value of individual differences between members in any group they may belong to.

Create family discussions or ask direct questions about classmates or teammates who may have learning, intellectual, or physical differences that cause others to tease. Ask how these events are perceived by classmates and affected students at their school or club and what they could do to change the culture. Offer factual information to your child about disabilities and teach your child that people have differences on the inside as well that must be accommodated in some way.

CHAPTER 6

Core Principle 5: Setting Boundaries and Consisten

Setting boundaries and consistent, loving discipline is the fifth principle of the five core principles of raising compassionate children. From the tiniest babies to the rowdiest teenagers, kids need boundaries—for their own moral and social development. Without clear limits, guidance, and appropriate consequences for bad choices, children will have a very difficult time learning right from wrong. They won't feel responsible for their actions, won't develop empathy for others, and won't be able to overcome adversity.

However, too much discipline is not ideal either. Discipline that is over-the-top or just plain unfair can damage kids emotionally and turn them into bullies or frequent targets of schoolyard bullying. The use of physical force or the demonization of kids can increase their likelihood of delinquency or even criminal behavior.

The best discipline is firm but fair, and clear in its limits. Kids should know what to expect if they break the rules. Let them know why these rules are in place—because you love them and want them to be safe and to grow up to be responsible and caring members of society. Childcare experts recommend discussing and agreeing on appropriate rules and consequences with your kids, adjusting them as they get older and can manage more responsibility.

Balancing Firmness with Understanding

Good parenting, according to Dr. Darcia Narvaez, a psychologist at the University of Notre Dame, is not about "controlling children so they can be orderly and appear successful." Rather, as she writes in *Psychology Today*, the goal is to motivate and guide them in ways that stimulate good internal drives to function well harmoniously. A big part of achieving that is balancing firmness with understanding. Parents need rules and should be parents and not friends, but children/grandchildren learn from experience. By helping children learn to make good choices through kind firmness, they can learn to be compassionate with themselves and others, and be better fit for community living and self-actualization.

Dr. Narvaez and her team have put together "The 5 Core Principles of Parenting" to foster compassionate children, which are based on such understandings of human nature.

A fine line to tread in parenting is setting boundaries and discipline while being compassionate, says Vivian Diller, Ph.D., a psychologist in private practice in New York City, where she works with families. "The best way to do that is through discipline," which provides children with guidelines or regulation, she says. "By setting limits, we teach them values, empathy, thinking before acting, consequences," she says, "all of which is included in compassion. We also teach self-control, which is necessary to curb anger and tune into the feelings of others. In other words, the very will and cognitive skills necessary to be compassionate are the very skills and intentions learned when given limits and eventually learning from their own mistakes, and successes." Parents must develop good judgment about boundaries, she adds. A parent should ask themselves if a rule is reasonable, and if it is being enforced in a reasonable way.

CHAPTER 7

The Role of Communication in Compassionate Parenti

Communication: It's how we tell the people around us that we love and understand them. Helping children develop effective communication skills benefits them beyond knowing how to effectively articulate their thoughts and feelings. It teaches them to actively listen to others' ideas and emotions, empathize with them, and speak up for those whose voices are too little to be heard. This is the key to compassionate collaboration that goes beyond leveraging power and fear to gain followers and into hearts being opened.

In a world where compassion is often considered a weakness, we cannot lead children to find the strength that comes from showing it without understanding the very basics of ethical dialogue, nor can we expect it to be initiated without imitating it. You want to raise kids who feel entitled to respect others, who want to talk to people when they are in pain and treat them with kindness. Mary Gordon, founder of the Roots of Empathy, tells parents, "Unless your children are good communicators, it's very hard to do that." According to psychoeducational consultant Michele Borba, "kindness, caring, empathetic children are also good communicators." Conversely, she says, "If your child is unable to communicate or listen to someone else's views, how could she possibly communicate compassion or listen to someone in need?" A strong core principle of compassionate communication is that the parent or educator believes that the child has the ability to develop such a level of competence, ethically.

Active Listening and Open Dialogue

Parents can foster compassion in children by providing open dialogue and actively listening to their problems and comments. Active listening involves hearing and truly understanding what the other person says. This also means that we should not judge what has been said until we have a firm understanding of what the other person is attempting to communicate. When listening, remember that listening includes open and nonverbal communication. Sometimes we pick up emotions by the way a person slouches or turns away when we speak. Active listening also involves responding. After hearing what a person says, it is often advisable to affirm what has been said before expressing opinions or reaching mutual understandings.

Non-verbal listening with children involves making eye contact, listening to what the child is saying, and acknowledging the child's contribution. It's also about giving the child time to say what's on their mind. This form of listening can open up a space for trust to develop between the parent and the child and help children develop a sense of empathy when the listener is an empathic or sensitive listener. With verbal or nonverbal communication, children (as well as adults) can feel when others express their feelings and reflect them back at that moment through their nonverbal gestures.

Active listening is a good tool for talking to children, plus it's a great way to build better communication with them. Not only do you offer your child a chance to talk about what's on their mind, but it will help you identify any issues that may need addressing. It tells children that they are important. Children learn better by doing, and communicating actively with them provides a good model for parenting. A parent's reaction to a child's communication (be it positive or negative) will illustrate to the child how they should behave when they want to communicate with others in the future.

CHAPTER 8

Cultivating Resilience and Self-Compassion in Chil

Two important constructs beneficial for mental and emotional well-being are resilience and self-compassion. Resilience is the ability to bounce back after being knocked down, to overcome adversity or challenges, and to develop grit or a growth mindset. It represents the courage and strength to tolerate and move through the discomfort of a situation. In children, resilience has a very close relationship with problem-solving ability.

Growing evidence suggests that self-compassion, described as kindness turned inward as we give ourselves the same caring responses that we offer to friends, is related to general social competence, overall adjustment, and fewer symptoms of anxiety and depression. It helps both in acknowledging the discomfort and in encouraging oneself to face the situation. Cultivating resilience and self-compassion in children is indeed a perfect match to the principle of parenting with compassion. The question arises as to how we can cultivate these two traits in children. Parents are the prime socializing agents and can greatly influence the development of these two important virtues. Here are a few ways in which parents can work on these capacities in children:

1. **Foster a Growth Mindset**: Teach that obstacles are opportunities to grow and develop, not threats.
2. **Let Them Solve Problems**: Instead of solving problems for them, let them feel failure at first and then help them find solutions themselves.
3. **Model Self-Compassion**: Show a self-compassionate attitude toward oneself when facing personal inadequacies.
4. **Encourage Strength Identification**: Encourage children to identify their strengths. Being aware of and having confidence in one's abilities helps to bring about a resilient response, which will curtail feelings of helplessness.
5. **Model a Growth Mindset Problem-Solving Approach**: Demonstrate how to approach problems with a growth mindset.
6. **Nurture Self-Compassion**: Encourage children to be their own best friends.

Building a Growth Mindset

Children are constantly bombarded with messages about being the best—getting good grades or excelling in activities. Child psychiatrists and psychologists warn about the mental health burden of trying to be perfect. Raising children to have a growth mindset has the potential to be one of the greatest gifts a parent can offer.

Dr. Kristin Neff, a leading researcher in self-compassion, examined how people would persevere or give up on an unsolvable anagram. What she found is that people who had a fixed mindset and made internal attributions blamed themselves for not being able to solve the puzzle. Those with a growth mindset, or a belief that they would do better the next time, tried harder and were resilient in the face of setbacks.

Growth mindset enthusiasts, such as Carol S. Dweck, a researcher at Stanford University, identified that children with a "fixed" mindset believed their intelligence was just a fixed trait where they had little control over the outcomes. Such children may often feel like they have something to prove. But children with a growth mindset, in contrast, perceive talents and abilities as starting points. They believe that through dedication, hard work, and effort, they could achieve their full potential. Dweck understands that essentially, the power of "yet" and acknowledgment of present struggles (which leads toward a growth mindset) is an act of self-compassion.

Cultivating a growth mindset in adults is something beautiful and powerful, so why not start in childhood? Teaching them the different meanings of failure, preparation, possibility, opportunity, and letdowns will help them develop resilience and self-compassion.

CHAPTER 9

Navigating Challenges and Obstacles in Parenting w

Just as peace is not merely the absence of war, compassion is not simply the absence of cruelty or suffering. When faced with challenges, as we all experience from time to time, compassion also involves respectful understanding, kindness, and even genuine warmth. It allows us to respect another person's "instinct for happiness" as the Dalai Lama describes - something we share from the moment we are born. This is a very important point to consider in raising our kids. When we address problems our children have with others - from mild teasing to more extreme bullying - it's very easy to get into a war with your kids and see compassion for others as nothing more than surrender. This is far from the case, however. True compassion involves empathizing with your child, but also respectfully understanding what might be causing others to act cruelly. You have to be careful to talk about the reasons behind cruel actions by others in a way that doesn't make your kid feel responsible for the way they are being treated. Instead, you are giving them a much more balanced view of what might be really going on.

Why is therapy so appealing - especially for kids? The answer is simple: we long to be heard and respected. We long for empathy. Every time you feel your own compassionate instincts taking a back seat, imagine you're a five-year-old child being treated unfairly by a friend who's betrayed your trust or a twelve-year-old girl in the eighth grade trying desperately to match her unique, ever-changing, svelte body to the impossible, static images of beauty that bombard her day after day. A lot of times this is exactly what our kids need us to do: to walk in their shoes or, better yet, just listen to their experience, without trying to "fix" or solve anything. Taking the time to listen without judgment to these concerns creates a safe space for children to become more resilient. If your child doesn't feel heard, they will struggle to be open to what you have to say.

Dealing with Bullying and Peer Pressure

Today, bullying isn't limited to physical aggression. It can be delivered through the internet and perpetuated through exclusion, rumor-spreading, and cyberbullying. One in four young children reports having been a victim of such attacks. Every responsible parent is justifiably alarmed at such a prospect. But our natural impulse to protect can go too far as we imagine instances of ridicule or aggression our children might face. We can catastrophize, becoming overprotective and undermining our children's resilience.

Parents often fret about how to prevent bullying, but they might not think about how to help children process it and move on after the fact. How much do your child's friendships mean to their happiness? How do they feel when they see someone else being bullied, teased, or left out? There is one skill action that underpins all of the other actions your child might choose from these connections, and that is the action of empathy - putting themselves in someone else's shoes. Letting your child's empathy guide their actions will go a long way towards them making kind and compassionate choices. Communicating clear values, such as the importance of community, generosity, pressing back against exclusion, etc., is important. It is nice to remind your child in tense moments of a particular value (and often effective, too: "What would you do if somebody pushed your friend?").

CHAPTER 10

Celebrating Diversity and Promoting Inclusivity in

As parents, we need to start talking about and exposing our children to all the shades of meaning, emotion, and perception that make up our vastly diverse human experience. Whether it's the stories and traditions of people from different faith backgrounds, or education about the lives of people of different races, genders, or sexual orientations, embracing diversity and inclusivity directly shifts us towards raising kids who can advocate for themselves and who will look to include others. Here are five ways parents can work on these principles:

1. **Model Being a Good Neighbor**:
    - Get to know people who are different from you and ask them about their experiences. Find out about different traditions and celebrations that go on in your local community.
    - Share your stories and family heritage with your kids. Visit culturally and ethnically diverse places.

- At festivals or special events, you can learn about and appreciate different foods, games, art, dances, and music.
- You'll also find out interesting things about people, families, and traditions in your community.
2. **Develop the 3 D's - Dialogue, Difference, Dignity**:
    - Believe that every child born in this world, like every adult, is a valuable human being with the potential to give and make a meaningful contribution to his or her community.
    - To raise kids who thrive and make a positive difference in the world, they need substantial exposure to difference, and the opportunity to develop a respectful and complex understanding of themselves and others.
3. **Find Out Who Your Neighbors Are**:
    - Help your kids accept the world in all of its diversity, and give your children authentic opportunities to know people from different cultures.

Exploring Different Cultures and Traditions

We don't have to look further than the tumultuous events of 2021 to see that our society remains fraught with deep divisions, some of which have led to considerable hostility and unrest. Naturally, this presents an interesting challenge for parents who strive to raise children that are understanding and compassionate. Preparing your children to navigate a pluralistic world begins by undergirding inclusivity at a young age within the family unit. The principles discussed in this section aim to expose your children to a diverse array of cultural experiences. The result is that children will gain insight into the lives, views, and customs of others—a first step toward developing empathy and compassion for individuals from across the globe.

One of the most effective ways to teach your children to be empathetic individuals is by showing through your actions that you esteem a diverse group of people and enjoy interacting with them. Don't stop yourself from appreciating people who are different from you, and don't try to hide it from your children. In fact, when you admire someone for their different way of seeing the world, tell them you do. If your praise is high enough, the child will often engage in a conversation with the person about their culture or tradition. This is a simple and easy way to bridge the gap between the different cultures found in your various communities.

Additionally, making your children more aware of what's happening around the world by watching the news, reading the newspaper, or internet blogs can help to build your child as a global citizen. By being more conversant with what's going on in the world, it can make your child become more aware of the issues their peers in other countries are going through.

CHAPTER 11

The Importance of Self-Care for Parents in Raising

Self-care is essential for parents aiming to raise compassionate kids. The more you care for your own well-being, the better you can care for your kid's well-being. Your calm demeanor will act as a calming signal to your child. Prioritizing how you are perceived as a parent over your child's actual feelings and needs will hinder your ability to help your child connect and be compassionate toward others.

Prioritizing Mental and Physical Well-Being

As a dedicated parent, you want the best for your children. In an age of immense cultural and social change, it can be difficult to guide children in the directions that will most benefit them and their success in life. Despite all of this change, the dual objectives of raising caring kids and promoting their social, emotional, and moral well-being have remained largely constant across generations. Fortunately, research suggests that parents can affect positive change, enhancing kids' birthrights to fulfill their potential as compassionate, caring individuals. To be optimally effective, a fundamental precondition of compassionate parenting is parents' prioritizing their own mental and physical well-being.

Your mental and physical well-being is the precursor to your ability to foster strengths and become a role model for compassion in your child's life. When you are well, you embody a model of mental wellness that can communicate compassionate, empathic concern. In this way, bibliotherapeutic, psychoeducational approaches teach parents to self-care so they can act effectively and compassionately. By intentionally increasing their own levels of well-being, parents can help shape their children's healthy social, emotional, and even financial future.

Focusing on your own mental and physical health when your kids are struggling and in pain can seem near impossible, yet compassion is not a depletable resource. Research suggests that parents who follow compassionate caregiving practices decrease their risk for relapse and experience fewer depressive and anxious symptoms even while in the acute stage of a major depression episode. Studies indicate that when parents practice strength-based interventions and intentionally choose to increase their own well-being, they benefit in many ways and as a result, their children seem to benefit as well. In the end, children raised by parents trained in compassion become open to learning compassionate ways of being.

CHAPTER 12

Conclusion: Embracing the Journey of Compassionate

For Shannon Hough, the practice of compassionate parenting cannot be distilled down to just one thing or quality. In the many interrelated decisions, interactions, attitudes, and skills it conveys, parenting itself becomes a creative exercise in what compassion can look like. This revolves around instilling values and seeking out opportunities to grow kinder and closer, making beauty, love, and fun. In many and sometimes redundant ways, the five core principles of compassionate parenting are highlighted, favoring a holistic rather than an atomistic focus. Indeed, instilling values is a work that is never completely done; for the parent who chooses it, compassion is a lifelong project.

The practice of guiding and nurturing that unfolds in compassionate parenting is the subject of this essay, tracing core principles through the obligations and attitudes it implies for parents. Such a parenting style turns the very process of child-rearing into a commitment to the compassionate fostering of great humans. By looking at the co-creation of a shared life and working to cultivate values, the history of parenting and, more broadly, the patient and gentle goal of turning participants into new and better people is depicted. Relational and attentive, compassionate parenting permits few generalizations about what your child needs in your interaction with them for one reason: that all people (even little ones) are unique, and what they require to grow into models of genuine beauty cannot be codified into step-by-step instructions.

Embracing the journey of compassionate parenting is about understanding that it's a continuous and evolving process. It's about being open to learning, growing, and adapting as both you and your child navigate through life together. Each interaction and decision you make lays the foundation for a compassionate future, not just for your child, but for the world they will help shape.

www.ingramcontent.com/pod-product-compliance
Lightning Source LLC
LaVergne TN
LVHW092100060526
838201LV00047B/1497